WOMEN
of the
CIVIL WAR

by Joan Nichols

Editorial Offices: Glenview, Illinois • Parsippany, New Jersey • New York, New York

Sales Offices: Needham, Massachusetts • Duluth, Georgia • Glenview, Illinois
Coppell, Texas • Sacramento, California • Mesa, Arizona

The Abolitionists

Some women were abolitionists before the Civil War even began. They wrote against slavery and spoke out in public speeches.

Sarah and Angelina Grimke were abolitionists who came from a family of wealthy slave owners in South Carolina. Yet they always believed all people were created equal.

Even as a child, Sarah Grimke hated slavery.

Angelina Grimke was Sarah's younger sister.

The Grimke sisters moved to the North and spoke out against slavery. The sisters were criticized by many people who believed that women should not give speeches in public. Other people admired these former slave owners who spoke out so strongly against slavery.

Sojourner Truth was born an enslaved person. She was tall, intelligent, and had a strong voice. When she spoke about her own experience at anti-slavery meetings, listeners were drawn to her powerful speaking.

3

When President Abraham Lincoln met Harriet Beecher Stowe, he supposedly said, "So you're the little woman who wrote the book that started this Great War!"

Two Harriets

Harriet Beecher Stowe was born in 1811 in Connecticut, which was a free state. In 1832 she moved to Ohio, which was also a free state at that time. Here Stowe learned about slavery and enslaved people who escaped to freedom.

She heard about a young African American woman who carried her baby across the river when it was covered with ice. Stowe used this story when she wrote *Uncle Tom's Cabin*. Her book made readers see enslaved people as fellow human beings.

The Woman Behind the Song

You may have heard the song that begins, "Mine eyes have seen the glory." Julia Ward Howe wrote it after she had heard some Union soldiers singing a popular marching song called "John Brown's Body." The next day she wrote new words for the song and sent them to *The Atlantic Monthly* magazine. Soon "The Battle Hymn of the Republic" was sung all over the North.

Most abolitionists spoke in public and wrote books to fight slavery. Harriet Tubman risked her own life and freedom to help enslaved people escape. She traveled south eighteen times, leading people north to freedom. Slave owners offered a large reward for her capture, but she was never caught.

Harriet Tubman, who was born an enslaved person, escaped in 1849. She was so thrilled to reach free ground, she said, "I looked at my hands to see if I were the same person."

The War at Home

After the South **seceded** from the Union in 1861, the fighting started. Women worked hard and acted with courage defending their homes and supporting the cause in which they believed.

Because most men in the North and South joined the army or were called up by the **draft**, women had to run the farms and businesses. Times were hard and there was a lack of food and clothing, especially in the South. Poor women went to work to support their families. Women also sent the soldiers blankets, sheets, towels, and food.

During the Civil War, nurses often worked with army officers.

Nurses

More than two thousand women served as nurses during the Civil War. Ellon McCormick Looby and her four-year-old son traveled from New York to Virginia to nurse her husband. She continued serving as a nurse in the same hospital until the war ended.

Clara Barton

Clara Barton decided to ask people to send her food and medical supplies for Union soldiers. Friends helped her deliver them to the battlefields. She also helped find missing soldiers and helped their families contact them. Later she founded the American Red Cross.

Sally Louisa Tompkins

Sally Louisa Tompkins opened a hospital in a friend's house in Richmond, Virginia. She used her own money to run it. Because the wounded soldiers got better, the army made her a captain. From then on she was called "Captain Sally."

Louisa May Alcott

Susie King Taylor

Mary Edwards Walker

A Writer and Nurse

The book *Little Women* takes place during the Civil War. Louisa May Alcott wrote it. In 1862 she went to Washington, D.C., to help take care of wounded soldiers. A month later Alcott got sick and had to return home. She wrote about her experiences in a book called *Hospital Sketches.*

Laundress, Teacher, Nurse

Susie King Taylor was born an enslaved person, but she learned how to read and write. When she was fourteen, she was freed by Union troops before slavery ended. She married Sergeant Edward King, a member of the 33rd United States Colored Troops. The 33rd was a **regiment** of former slaves.

Taylor lived with the regiment. She taught the soldiers how to read and write. She nursed the wounded and continued working as a nurse for the next four years.

Woman Doctor in the War

Dr. Mary Edwards Walker was the first woman doctor to serve in the Union army. She was later appointed as a medical officer. She was captured by the Confederates in 1864 and spent four months in prison. After the war she was given the Congressional Medal of Honor, the country's highest military award. She was the first woman ever to receive it.

Spies

Some women became spies for the North or for the South. They found out the enemy's important secrets and told these secrets to leaders on their own side. Some women were **couriers**, or people who carried messages across enemy lines.

Rose O'Neal Greenhow

Rose O'Neal Greenhow had many important friends in Washington, D.C., so she was able to get information from them secretly. She then told the Confederate army what information she learned.

Rose O'Neal Greenhow

Elizabeth Van Lew

Elizabeth Van Lew

Elizabeth Van Lew was a Southerner who spied for the North. She pretended to bring gifts to Union prisoners in Richmond, Virginia. Actually, the prisoners gave her information. They sometimes used a code she invented.

Sarah Emma Edmonds served in the Union army as "Franklin Thompson."

Soldiers

At least four hundred women dressed as men and joined the armies of the North and the South. Some joined to be with their husbands or brothers. Many served because they strongly believed in their side's cause. Others went just for the adventure. Most of these women soldiers were found out only when they became ill or wounded.

Loreta Velazquez served in the Confederate army as "Lt. Harry T. Buford." She wore a false beard and mustache.

Teachers

When Union soldiers entered the South, enslaved people followed them. Besides wanting to be free, the enslaved people also needed food, shelter, jobs, and medical care. They also wanted to learn. Northern men and women came south to help them, and many of the women became teachers.

This picture shows a school in Vicksburg, Mississippi, for former enslaved people.

Charlotte Forten

Charlotte Forten, a free African American, had a good education and joined the abolitionist movement. She became a teacher and wanted to help enslaved people. She taught on St. Helena Island, South Carolina.

Glossary

courier a messenger

draft a law that requires men of a certain age to serve in the military, if called

regiment an army group with a large number of soldiers

secede to break away from a group, as the Southern states broke away from the United States